Edited by Tanisha Bodden &
NeFesha Yisra'el

emerge

By Huldah Dauid

Illustrations by Daryna Kurinna

emerge

Huldah Shlomit Dauid/Royal Roots Publishing
www.Huldahdauid.com
Info@allthingsroyalroots.com

Emerge/ Huldah Shlomit Dauid – 1st ed.
ISBN: 978-1-7337520-7-7

Other poetry books by Huldah Dauid
Her Peace of Mind

To my Creator and Savior
who proved that He is there even in the shadow

INTRODUCTION

EMERGENCE IN THE BEGINNING

Emerge is a work dedicated to helping the reader find self through the process of journeying into the dark and emerging whole. One of the most beautiful symbols in nature is the white lotus. It sits beautifully upon its throne with roots submerged into darkness. Its purity is a stark contrast to the depths from which it comes. It is an alluring reminder that refinement can come out of ghastly circumstances. It is the aide-memoire that from darkness, the light comes forth. This has been the message from the beginning of time.

In Genesis 1:2, the bible states that "the earth was without form and void and darkness was on the surface of the abyss." It is from the formless and empty space that light is called forth. Light is told to "be," and it is. Light is given the assignment to emerge and bring order to chaos. Each of us is on a similar journey to continually come forth and shine, but to do so, we must understand the darkness surrounding us and the darkness within. This process takes introspection, confrontation, faith, and an abundance of love.

The book of Genesis continues with a story of a man named Adam. Adam is said to be formed from the dust of the ground in the likeness and image of Elohim. He is pressed together using the same ground which sat beneath the waters in the darkness. This submerged ground becomes the medium through which the Master Potter takes clay to fashion a man that will reflect the power of the Divine. Adam is placed into a paradise, and while there, he reflects on creation. As he mindfully observes his environment of abundance, Adam experiences feelings of lack. Each created being has someone who epitomizes their essence, and there is no one for Adam. Adam doesn't see that he is made to reflect his Maker, so Elohim gives Adam that opportunity to see Self. For Adam to understand his role, he must actualize, and the only way to actualize is through seeing what is within. Elohim doesn't give Adam something from without to fulfil his desire; instead, he draws from Adam. Adam is split open, and Elohim uses Adam's feminine side as the framework for his physical counterpart. He literally receives "bone of his bone and flesh of his flesh," in the feminine. This concept is similar to Carl Jung's psychoanalytic theory concerning collective consciousness. Jun-gian theory states that the psyche comprises feminine and masculine parts called the anima and animus. This woman is the animus of Adam who came from the Adamah (ground (feminine)). A beautiful linguistic combination adds concrete understanding to the spiritual, psychological, and physical hu-man experience.

As the story continues, the woman stands before him as his equal opposite and mirrors him himself. He is faced with temptation, lust/desire, grief, divorce, and ultimately love through her. She becomes his biggest challenge and his greatest passion. In the process of their separation from paradise, they learn to use their different functions and abilities to become one. In their knowledge of self and one another, they find their way back to the Divine. The story of Adam and Chavah can be seen as a conscious descent into the darkness of duality. To overcome, they must labor in the fields of the unknown to join back into one. In this way, their lives serve as a template for overcoming the knowledge of "good and evil," which has been deposited into our minds through diverse lived experiences. Through experience and knowledge, yielded to the Infinite, we also find themselves and repair the brokenness caused by our duality. As each person on their journey to heal-disparate reconciles those parts, they begin to become one with self and the Divine.

EMERGENCE & THE SHADOW

Many people might ask why darkness? The absence of light is a scary theme in the world. It is a place of unknown, but it is also a fertile void. Estelle Frankel, the author of The Wisdom of Not Knowing, calls darkness "the fertile void." It is a place of infinite unactualized, and unseen possibilities. Darkness can hold unnerving phenomena, but it can also possess endless possibilities and beauty. From the dark waters of the mind, we can bring forth good, and from the same space, dysfunction can arise. It is only in acquaintance with this shadowy space that we thrive. The psychoanalyst Carl Jung, best known for his work on the shadow archetype provides a blueprint in his work regarding healing the inner self. The shadow is the subconscious mind made up of both positive and negative experiences that require elucidation to progress from one stage of development to another. The shadow, if suppressed, can create projections that cause conscious complexities. The mind becomes disunited if the shadow is not encountered, merged, and assimilated. Assimilation of the shadow is not identification with darkness; instead, it is conscious awareness of a multifaceted personal experience. Carl Jung teaches that there is no certainty of emergence from the spirals of the subconscious. There must be a continuous baptism and re-emergence through introspection and deep inner work to "become." This process is highlighted in the biblical text as humanity is required to stand face to face with a higher Being and His law to receive the ritual of integration. Each cultural practice of the ancient Hebrews represents an invitation to part with the divided psyche and embody love and God's divine nature. It is a beckoning away from the duality, "good and evil" and black and white thinking, into a space of illumination. A place where a gentle lamp lights the way through the darkness. A place where one is no longer afraid of what lurks in the shadows.

Emerge is a work of individuation—creating a mediation between the instinctual desires of the id and the critical superego. The birthing waters of the mind form an integrated version of divided relationships and psyche. Emerge is a talk with self, humanity, and an effort to gather the traumatized fragments deposited into subconscious darkness to a singular space to be seen and heard. It is the cry of the infant inside asking to be rescued from the confines of helplessness but realizing that weaning from parental arms to self-soothing is a part of the healing process. It teaches sacrifice without loss. It divorces the persona for wholeness and the mask for the authentic visage. Each poem and thought are a glimpse into the darkness. It is a glimpse into a grave. A plunge into a universal psyche because we are all a part of a collective experience. But most importantly, this anthology is an emergence from the womb of healing into the arms of divine love and beautiful restoration.

I realized that everything I experienced was due to my darkness

I could not be abused without the propensity to allow it

My wounds brought the sharks

My death brought the vultures

My lack of trust in Yah caused my insecurity

I became both the darkness and the light

And depending on the darkness in others

My pain would draw them like a moth to a flame

I learned that I fawn for my abusers

And punish me when they discard me

I feed the insecurities of others

Hoping they will return the favor

I can be a masochist and a fatal attraction

The fire consumes me

And I also set things ablaze

I am the wise gardener

And the sower of dissent

into my fruitful vineyard

It was through this confrontation

that I was buried

And reborn

No longer dual but embracing all of who I am

I am my past and my future

Called to refinement by my present

I am me

Ever-changing

Merging my duality

Submitting my brokenness to my Creator

No longer craving

No longer running

Rising from the murky waters

A white lotus

emerging

GRIEF

Pain is caused when grief creates a hole in wholeness. When a sizable wound is חלה
made in the body, it affects the immune system. The injury, if left untreated,
can become infected. This causes the body to be in a state of dis-ease, and the
body will eventually shut down unless there is intervention and healing. In like
manner, a grief wound, if left untreated, can "infect" a person mentally,
physically, and emotionally. Grief may manifest physically but requires a
layered approach to achieve wholeness. This process is spiritual, emotional, and
mental.

When a person grieves, they enter a state of sorrow and heaviness. Their minds יגה
vex them, causing physical and mental symptoms. The suffering felt in grief
can be so heavy that they feel tormented. These feelings can be crippling,
causing them to freeze and feel afraid amid the affliction.

Grief is a type of suffering that is bigger than emotional hurt. Grief is felt both כאב
within and without. This compound sorrow is seen as a marring that requires
intervention. When the body is hurt, biological systems come to its aid,
repairing breaches, and providing coverage to gaping wounds. Spiritually there
is a remedy for grief—a divine sacrifice for the covering of the hole. A blood
ritual that is applied as the physician's balm to the wound of the psyche
provides true healing. At the end of any significant recovery, a scar remains,
but the mind is wiped clean by the anesthesia of salvation.

Untended grief grows into rage and anger. The rage and anger are not the כעס
enemies but rather the alarm of the soul signaling a need for healing.
Indignation grows like weeds in the fertile ground of a broken heart leading to
anxiousness and vexation. The grief from lost opportunities, unfulfilled
expectations, and rejection is the cause of deep annoyance, frustration, and
worry. This Hebrew word gives language to the sore and sorrowful heart that is
signaling a need for relief but is enraged at having symptoms with no healing
practitioner.

There must be change or exchange for the triune man to heal from grief. An מור
exchange of the bitter tears of despair to the joy of living water. When the
waters of grief refuse to flow, bitterness festers in the inner man. For the
stagnant pools to be purified, tears must be released. Tears bitter to the taste
clean the heart's well for living water to flow. The headwaters are renewed
through the soul lament, and grief turns to joy. Only the rebellious heart will
keep back the bitter waters denying the soul its due transformation.

Challah (הלח) is the Hebrew word for a portion. On Shabbat, many Jews create a loaf of bread and set aside a piece of dough to symbolize the levitical heave offering "For G-d" (Num.15:20). This process of bread making is a ritual of sorts for me to release, pause, and exercise patience. The bread goes through a process of perfection for my family's table, which is synonymous with the process I go through spiritually as I prepare to offer myself to the Creator in rested communion. So what do bread and grief have to do with one another?

During this season of intense grief, so many of my "ritual" practices were left out of Shabbat. Most weeks leading to the Sabbath, I was just grateful to survive. The suffering I have felt at times while merging my duality was so intense that I could barely light candles and pray. The amount of pain I felt from guilt and shame weighed me down. I was pierced through with pain. Grief weakened my immune system. It brought illness into my home physically, mentally, and emotionally. I tried everything to pacify and ease the pain. The more I tried, the worst I got. For me, grief caused me to hold on to things that would taint the finished product. Grief was driven by ego and pride that I could not let go of. I wanted to be made new but was not yielding to the process. I would not submit to the rise and fall necessary to be whole. I was holding on to a portion that was not mine. I had to surrender and waive the grief piece for my peace. But surrender requires trust, and I struggled to trust G-d with my brokenness.

While I was hurt and grieving, I was convinced that grief was the totality of my existence, and my fragmented sanity was all I would ever have left. But I have learned that grief is the portion surrendered. It is not a hole to cause hurt but a removal that, if dealt with, can lead to healing and wisdom;

A bit removed as a testament of the toil and threshing—an offering after coming from the threshing floor. In Numbers 15:20, my ancestors were commanded to make a cake after their harvests and given as firstfruits to Hashem. The same word for this cake (challah) is also grief. In letting go of the past, I understood the principle in the heave-offering. I learned to give my grief to G-d; it is His portion after the toil. It shows that I have gone through the process and trusted him to make me whole.

It is only in practice that we understand the principle. Without the ritual process, one will never understand the joy of the rite. I have a new understanding of my year and my grief. I look at the beautiful rituals in my cultural practices and have learned the beauty of a loaf of bread. In this practice, I release the pain in the rhythm of kneading. I separate the dough and braid it into a single loaf, reminded that everything works together for good. As I place the loaf in the oven, I will praise the Holy One, blessed be He, for the ability to be tried in the fire. And at last, as the table is set and my loved ones sit in anticipation of a meal, I remember that this process of my healing was not to break us apart but to draw us together. We will not forget how He restored us after the toil at the threshing floor as we bless the bread.

בָּרוּךְ אַתָּה, יְיָ אֱלֹהֵינוּ, מֶלֶךְ הָעוֹלָם הַמּוֹצִיא לֶחֶם מִן הָאָרֶץ.

Baruch atah, Yah
Eloheinu melech ha olam,
hamotzi lechem min ha aretz.

Blessed are You, Yah our Elohim, King of the universe, who brings
forth bread from the earth.

It's like sorrow is in my DNA

I'm Epigenetically attached to my trauma

Cold weather
Pumpkin spice
Bites in the breeze
Reminding me of the transition loss brings

I lost me in this season before
The ghost of my former self breathes her chilling breath on me

Cold bodies
A graveyard in my soul

An empty cavity
Zombie
Walking dead
Missing heartbeats

Frozen in time

To heal is to feel
The rage
       The sorrow
The joy
       The loss

I have only healed from you when I have felt you deeply

I will feel much better when the wound of today

Becomes the scar of tomorrow

Always a healer

But

Never healed

I have cried for you

But I have yet

To cry for myself

I am on the threshing floor
When I look around all I see is chaff

You plowed into my virgin soil

Planted your seeds

I yielded a bountiful harvest

And you never amended the soil

All I have left is dirt

My tears are my teacher
They sting as they hit my wounds
They remind me of the pain
When my mind forgets

Grief is temporary

The hole will become whole

Pain is a sign you are healing

Sometimes you visit me in my dreams
I see your face and you laugh
I see your figure but
I only know it's you when I awake
And you are not here

Rituals mark the grief

Dance the grief
Sing the grief
Write the grief
Soak out the grief
Take a pilgrimage and plant the grief

In whatever way you can release the grief
Take it to God's doorstep
So that you can unpackage and process the grief
Process the grief so that the weight of it is bearable
with time

Why do I hold back tears like clouds over the desert?
Doesn't the ground need the rain?
I must admit that I am afraid of what might grow
I don't want the sin-laden cacti that I may produce
I don't want the flash flood of emotional turmoil
that lies bottled up inside.
If I were safe, then my tears would fall delicately
onto parched ground
Gracefully descending like a spring shower
but the raging waters inside say otherwise
so I deny the healing
because I won't be able to stop the tears
once I begin crying

Give me space
Inches, feet, yards
Distance
Solitude, quiet, sanctuary

Space

To heal, to think, to breathe
Because I am suffocating! Constantly under
the time constraints of someone's needs
Stand back
Don't need me
Give me space

I pray

Sitting on what feels like the fringe of life and death

and holding on by a hair of sanity

Heavenly Father,

There must be a part of this story that is yet to be written.

I hope my pain in this moment is rehearsal

 for the joy to come

"You Will Find Your Song" -EF

there is no song so sweet and resonant
as one sung in hollow spaces
the amphitheater carved into the stone heart
waits to amplify an untold story
I stand on the stage
eyes peer into my soul
an expectant audience awaits
I open my mouth, and there is nothing but silence
(Voiceless)

I hear her whisper: "you will find your song."

Panicking! I try to sing the lyrics of others
but they just don't roll off the lips right
so, I stand under the spotlight in silence
tears streaming down my face
Where is my song?

the gentle voice reassures me,
"the unsung song comes forth
when the vessel is rid
of sound dampening suppression. Feel the pain!"

tears blur out my face

My throat is set ablaze

I let out a howl from the pit of my stomach

I begin humming to the walls of this tomb

waiting for an echo of hope from beyond

(Background singers)

I tap my feet to the rhythm of my wailing & moans

patting the ground enthusiastically anticipating

 mourning turned to dance

(percussion)

I pray in the diminished chords of a broken heart

adding colorful tonality to a melancholy soul

(Melody)

As I lean into the groove

my body begins to sway

like a woman moving through contractions

I realize my song was always there

it was just clashing

I was waiting for a ballad, but my soul sang the blues

(My song)

Sometimes I want to die
just to see if the solace is sweet

My heart aches of the little girls
Having to watch me heal my inner little girl
But I must become the mother I needed
So, they can have the mother they need

Every word of healing I speak to them
comes from a deep need to hear those words spoken
to the 8- and 10-year-old me

I find it to be no coincidence
that my deepest healing
is during the years when they are
the age of my deepest hurt

In so many ways
I feel like I have gone so far inward
Only to remain broken
Still locked within me

As I release myself from mental captivity
I am learning to let go of the expectations
and burdens I place on my children to bear me
to heal me through good behavior and academic performance
I was using their achievements as validation of my healing

Having children and employing them as agents for restoration
will only cause frustration
although they are in the world to bring healing
I must heal so they have the tools

As I struggle with the guilt of stealing their innocence
through divorce and perpetuating a trauma and stigma

I must rest in the reality
that my healing is the validity
they will need to step boldly
into every version of themselves

My heart aches as we cry over FaceTime calls
due to the distance of relational death
I must hope in the process and find joy in the promise
that this was not all in vain

DIVORCE

For I hate divorce, says Yah Elohim of Israel, because it
seeks to sweep the root causes under the rug, says Yah of
Hosts So in the protection of your life path do not
present false outer appearances.

Malachi 2:16

Shalach means to send away to or to move toward a goal. It is likened to being סְ/שׁלח
sent out to pasture with the rest of the herd instead of being kept close like the
choice lamb or sheep. When a woman is "sent," she is being released with
careful oversight. This type of divorce is a separation where love
struggles to override dysfunction. When ego and pain harden the heart it
becomes impossible to dwell together peaceably. In the bible, Elohim "sent"
Adam and Chavah from his presence because they violated the
stipulations of the garden. This word is not always negative because
Elohim intended to move Adam and Chavah to a goal. To be sent away from
one home does not always end in the finality of discard. When Yah is
allowed to do a work in the husband and the wife, the Creator requires the
eyes of the husband to join him in intimate oversight. Just as the shepherd
stands in the wilderness watching the flock, the husband watches
the one experiencing freedom or expulsion learning and allowing his
wife to be taught. Both parties are hoping for an exceptional outcome.
At the achievement of this goal and proper timing, a way is made for
reunion, renewal, and restoration.

גרש

Divorce removes status. This word is similar to the term above in that it carries
the ancient agrarian context of being sent out. The difference is this word
means to cast out. This Hebrew word for divorce means to lower class and
remove status. This type of individual is seen as a stranger or a traveler, and
they are without oversight. A person who experiences this type of divorce is
wholly dismissed from their duties. This gives room for replacement and can
result in a person returning to a lesser position than before they were sent or
left the marriage.

כרת

When a divorce is executed in finality it is likened to a fatal blow. When a
divorce is finalized, a person is cut off and cut out of the covenant. The woman
is cut off from her husband and is cut off from enjoying the benefits of being a
wife. The parties break covenant with families and people often become divided
in the process.

Last year I sat behind a camera before boarding a flight and announced that my marriage was over. Tears streamed down my face as I reflected on years of gaslighting, control, fighting, dysregulation, compounded with childhood trauma and unresolved personal darkness. I was tired, the baggage was too heavy, and it destroyed me, my children, and everyone close to me. I reached a point where the adversary had found my grievous wound, and he was going in for the kill. When I decided to leave, it was with much prayer, fasting, and council. I fasted for 40 days before I left. All I heard was, "go!" I believed in my heart that if I stayed another day, I would not make it out alive, and if I lived, I would lose my mind. I was in flight mode, and whether it was the God in my head or the Creator of all things, I will let you be the judge of that at the end of this segment but what I will tell you is that preservation of life rose above every dissenting thought within and without. I am using this section to share the beauty of divorce. I say the beauty because I was fortunate enough to experience the shalach (sending to a goal) of divorce and the beauty of restoration of myself and my family.

My divorce was not one of marital annihilation, but I divorced a victim mindset, divorced the helpless child narrative, and became a WOMAN, one who has the tools to set necessary boundaries, be tender, and submit to the will of the Creator continually. The poems in this section share my hurt, but more importantly, a journey from brokenness to wholistic submission. While the world may deny the change that can happen when Yah is in the midst, I stand witness that what looks like a catastrophe can become a catalyst for healing. While it may be difficult to see the blessing in the separation process, it is in service and true repentance before the Creator that we break generational curses and our hearts become fertile soil for our sake. Whether the restoration is a new heart or new love, to receive the benefit of brokenness, we must submit to Elohim so that He can do a work in us. A dear friend once told me that Yah is doing something marvelous in our eyes.

Divorce has called me to let go of so much, and I feel empty. I spent my marriage consuming; food, trips, and meaningless items to add value to my depleting self-worth. More to feel less, but consumption only masks the pain. A pill of sorts that covers symptoms of inner worthlessness. Then I came across a new perspective that challenged the core of my consumption. Minimalism. The thought that "less can be more." Living and doing with intention. A sort of mindful approach to managing the materialism that served as a way to mask my diminishing identity as I transition from overindulgence to intentionality. As I ponder building self-worth from within, I am beginning to see minimalism as a function over form, which resonates deeply with me on so many levels. I am learning that as a black woman, it is not what things look like from the inside but how healed I am inside. I need my worth to be intangible before I manifest in the physical. I need something that a change in relationship status or wages cannot affect. I feel like every crevice of my life needs minimalism, including my faith.

Growing up religious, I realized that I was also hiding behind spiritual overconsumption seeking approval from a God I believed wanted me to earn his love. If my marriage wasn't perfect, then I didn't really love God. So, I sacrificed my mental health and was overloaded with guilt and emotional abuse from myself and others. The quantity of my abuse was the measure of my holiness. I was hoarding hurt as a sign of my dedication to God. I have been bombarded with a plethora of beliefs and opinions about God, life, success, marriage, and family, which clutter my mind and trigger so much of my overconsumption. I have spent the last 12 years over-consuming knowledge, things, and experiences to conform to a religious system. This overconsumption has caused me to stifle my voice and Gods, who are heard from within first, contrary to popular belief. A still gentle voice cannot be heard amongst the roar of inner clutter and overstimulation.

I am spiritually, physically, and mentally overstimulated. Minimalism is not an option; it's a part of a divine call and becoming. I no longer wish to create a facade. Instead, I am journeying toward releasing, releasing to receive an abundance of the intangible. Minimalism is not just a journey of ridding of belongings but a journey toward loving self in authenticity. I am searching for a decluttered experience "within" as much as I am working to shed what is "without." Without peeling back, the layers of emotional, mental, and physical hoarding, I cannot journey within. Here I am, taking it all off to stand bare before myself so I can see the authentic contents of the Divine within.

#AssiduitytoAfromilimalism

Sometimes the key
that unlocks the door of your heart
is hidden
in the dungeon of the soul
dark journey
to be free

The magic that was yesterday
Is the sting of a scraped knee in the shower
My tears wash away the possibility fleetingly felt
Oh, love, why do you build me up so high
only to plunge me into the deepest depths

Am I a Lauryn Hill lyric on repeat?

I keep letting you back in/how can I explain myself/ as painful as
this thing has been/I just can't be with no one else

I feel like a revolving door

A city without walls

You are so good at tearing down my defenses

But I don't remember you helping build them back

I feel abandoned

I am so open

Vulnerable

You seem ignorant to my truth

Even though you don't speak my emotional language

It's how you get back in every time

Why do I write my pain?
Why do I share?
Because it hurts
So instead of slitting my wrist
I let my pen bleed

People don't tell you that divorce separates everything
It's not just cars and living quarters
Divorce also fractures time
Wholeness is now fragmented

I miss my children when they are gone
I don't know time without them
I don't know who I am without them
I have wrapped my identity in them, and now I must split them
I will only see half of their life
Maybe even less
Was this decision worth the sacrifice

But how much was I present when my mind was under attack
How many moments were lost that I will never get back
Maybe a few intentional moments is key
I can't engulf myself in them and risk losing me

I have abandonment issues
and I reinforce them every time
I leave me to pursue loving you

The Breakup

The break up is easy at the beginning

We want to get out, so we see all the bad

But time lessens the blow of the offenses

Then I begin to crave you

I want more of your abuse because at least it feels like something

The make-up comes with a high

Intense sex. Empty promises. Release of the tension that the divide brings

The breakup is easy at the beginning

It's easy to deny you when I have recently had you

But what happens when my nature churns within

The phone call is simple

The arrival is prompt

The sex is passionate, but the death is sure.

It breaks my heart that separating from you

is teaching my children that love is conditional

How can two people who love each other this much

fail to hold their love together

What a terrible lesson of impermanence

At least that's what's on the surface

Underneath I am in turmoil

I feel inadequate because of how I can never do anything right

My children are being taught through microaggressions to disrespect me

My children are being taught that I am weak

My children don't see my resilience they only see the mother who reacts

They only see the mother who has tear filled eyes

They don't see the silent dysfunction

They see the smile turned to frown

The behaviors they have been taught so subtly

They feel lost

What is happening on the inside is also on the outside

This hurts

I never admitted to loving you the way that I do. Loving you then would become the justification for my toleration of the dark parts of you.
Or is it my pity, my codependence, and my lack of boundaries

Or maybe
When they ask if I love you, they really just want the truth

Do I love you? Yes.

That is why I leave. Sounds strange. I know.

I know my love language is needy
I know it can be a foreign tongue and requires a translator
But when love is not given an ear
and when its distribution inequitable
It feels like a prison
And now I am clawing at freedoms door

I love you never came

Not even an I miss you? not even like an old friend?

Can I be honest about my feelings, at least with myself?

I must admit I am tired of loving someone who doesn't love me.
 Why is love wasted on the broken?

I had to be away from you to love you fully

I had to be away from you to love me

I had to be away from you to find wholeness

Now comes the hardest feat of it all

I must keep my wholeness away from you

I must refrain from the returning to the old versions of myself

That cause me to offer my love and wholeness as a ritual sacrifice

to a cult of brokenness

#shadowself

What about you not wanting me makes me crave you.
Chasing pain of rejection like a high
Stroking my ego when you play cat and mouse
this is a black hole, and, in the end, I lose
My dignity and eventually my soul

Your lips whisper thank you
but I am afraid to say you're welcome
welcome where and what will you do with this permission
If I allow you into my garden will you tend to it
will you see its fragility and offer protection

Do you know a delicate flower
or a tender plant when it is before you

Or are you harsh winds on fragrant petals
a scorching sun
to moist and fertile soil
struggling to blossom
in due season

Was the home we built ever permanent?

Or was it storage for traumas

a façade we created to hide the hurts neither of us could face

Go home wayward one

don't stray

How can I return home

when home was just a storage unit

for things neither of us could ever let go

The only option is to relocate our love

to find home in one another

and build anew

16751

I never got to love you fully
the wall to your heart was too hard to climb
wanting to love you felt like a suicide mission
but I persued it
and died a thousand times

When my endurance is questioned,
I invite you to look at the frost bite on my heart
Irreparable damage due to the cold I have endured
in the winter of our "love"

I never felt secure
the bounds were blurred
so I walked into the wide open

You abandoned me in my sorrow

a thousand times

before I ever said goodbye

our relationship
was a lesson
on saying
endless goodbyes

I will never stop loving you
I just refuse to allow my love
To keep shattering me

Our love was a glass house
and your unhealed little boy
doesn't know the gravity
of the rocks he threw

Why won't you love me
Not feeling your love is killing me

Why won't you love me
When the ease of loving me is fool proof
You don't have to work for my love
Everything I have is already yours

I am begging you to love me
give me permission to teach you my love

Dont refuse me
but if you won't love me
All that's left is to bury me
and accept these flower
from my grave

You are called to save souls
but you never saved me

you can pontificate
with grandiosity
but you never spoke to me

you studied foreign languages
and unlocked deep mysteries
hidden in ancient texts
But you didn't study me

All the while I waited
Loving you
Beyond space and time

I only wanted you
But it never seemed like you wanted me

I tried to wash you off my skin
I tried to drown out your words
But you have taken root in my soul

An infinite number of eyes on me

Never mattered

I was staring at you

Wait for you

To see me

Just once

I will stop crying when my tears

have washed away

every painful memory

Mourning death is easier
than the death of a relationship
Because in death
my heart has no room to hope

My body doesn't know another like I know you
The mold of my secret place has become
Your passage to distant worlds and fountain of immortality

My breasts have nourished your babies
My body with every line and crevice is evidence of you mining
diamonds from my womb

When I think about being with another I cringe because I look
in the mirror and even though it's just me reflected, I see your
cultivated garden
Whether barren or fruitful
Neglected or hedged
it is yours

you are responsible for this soil
you are called to tend it for your sake
you are supposed to restore and amend what has been depleted
by the sweat of your brow

263 days

I am still waiting for him to come to me
Not just come to me with an I'm sorry
But to rescue me

I need more than make up sex
I need a fire to burn all of the walls I built
I don't want lullabies
Instead I perfer long conversations
that leave us open and raw
Ready for something different
but, here we are dancing the tango
 while the relationship sinks

Aggressively tugging and pulling
against one another for change

This time like so many times before, I want him to come with
more, come with a plan of correction, come with open arms

But I am growing weary of waiting

I focus on fixing myself
Bargaining
and seeking a piece of peace

Oh the peace of hearing him say

I love you

I'm sorry

I have been getting help

this is what Yah has spoken to me

and this is what I am going to do:

I am going to pause my life for you; I will heal with you, I am going to hurt with you, and cry with you. I am going to restore you, restore us, restore our children. I will fall apart and trust Yah to put everything back together. I won't push through. I won't stop until all that is destroyed is rebuilt. You and my children need a wall, like the walls of Jerusalem, to protect you. I will be that. It's okay to fall apart here. You are my bride, and whether you are Gomer or Esther, I will love you until you are without spot or wrinkle. I will wash you in the word until you are blameless. You are adamah, and I am Adam, and I will toil by the sweat of my brow until you bear fruit. I realize that you are for my sake.

263 days I have waited. Yes, I have been resistant. Yes, I have grown a hedge of thorns. But why was he never the gentle gardener, like the Elohim and Savior I serve, who comes for the one?

I Have Heard It Over and Over Again

God hates divorce
It was given because of the hardness of your hearts
What God brings together let no man tear apart
A 3-strand cord is not easily broken
Love endures all things
The scriptures have spoken

Well, why does this hurt
Why am I crying
Why does "love" have me cheating and lying
The safety and comfort of covenant is lost
When ego and pride lead
The relationship is tempest
Our ship is tossed

Fighting back tears
I pack once again
Struggling with the reality that leaving you is sin
I don't want to go
Lord knows I want to stay
But I'll be damned if I do this one more day

My once tender heart

Beating Slower and slower

A pain and heaviness in my chest

From carrying a burden none can shoulder

I buckle beneath the weight

I force myself to leave

I can't love you when my mind is begging please

The cold and hollow cavity

Where love for you once dwelled

Is replaced with anger and malice

A hate unparalleled

I'll never kiss your lips

Or hum our favorite song

This was all a big mistake

A game played far too long

Hours turn into days

To months

A year soon past

Freedom, joy, renewal

Yet something holds me fast

With each new dawn

A gentle dew

With each new season rain

Former and latter

Pound the stone

And I can feel again

With those feelings a flashing flood

And I am here again

A garden laid barren

Is volunteering love again

The cycle of life

A mystery unparalleled

What went into the grave

Fertilizes what we know had surely failed

With new saplings taking root

 and seeds sown unbeknownst

I incline my ear to the small still voice

Your life is not your own

Like the bride awaits the groom

A bit anxious and afraid

Of a future soon to bloom

Just know my hand is there

What you can see

What you can control has never been my will

Put your wedding clothing on

Daughter of Sarah do you trust me still

Without a word

To some absurd

I'll wait a little more

A heart transplant and eyes on God

I'll wait a little more

ידע

KNOW

To know something is a process. It requires knowledge, thought, and an intimate experience/relationship with a person or environment. In modern society, we are led to believe we know something based upon intellect, having never had an intimate engagement with people or places due to technology. Yet nothing can take the place of empirical hands-on experience. Hebraically, to honestly know something, there has to be practice. The practice of differentiating thoughts, acknowledging truth, and being transformed by information is perfected through experience. The accurate measure of knowledge is to do and act in alignment with the depth of the transformational experience.

יָדַע

My daughters are the fierce expression
of every ounce of my suppression
they are wild & free
flame and fire

You both inherit
the purest part of my firey soul
Your hearts sincere desires
will never be quenched

My soul chants to thousands of ancestors

A hum and moan in a familiar tone

A warrior's cry intermingled with sorrow and tears

Waiting for a response, an acknowledgement, an invitation to re-
turn

From a distant land

My mind, along with my life, shattered into a million pieces
and I had to write myself back to safety
Grief carried me like a torrent wave
into the depths of the ocean
and I had two choices:
sink or swim

I chose the latter
I clawed through the salty water
Fatigue and tiredness overtook my body

I'm going to die out here

But then from the distance
I heard a faint chanting
A beckoning that vibrated deep within

The shore was lined
with women in white illuminated by the divine
Welcoming me to safety
Their wails and moans
Chanting and drumbeats
Helped me catch my rhythm

Flailing arms and uncoordinated legs caught the rhythm

I began to progress toward safety

The sound louder, and in that moment, I felt no more pain

I was being healed

When I arrived at the shore, they told me stories of how I was swept away

and how they came together and formed a healing circle

They told me that they prayed for me

They prayed that all that was heavy would drown at sea

and that the tender portion would return

They formed a circle

women who had journeyed before me

Those who have grieved love & youth

And they committed to being the mothers, aunties, and friends I would need as I rebuilt

As I lay collapsed on the shore

Breathing beginning to slow down

I realized I had entered the sacred womb of creation

A safe space

A divine feminine healing was about to take place

I pray you know a love deeper than the ocean
And that your head floats above
Cotton candy clouds

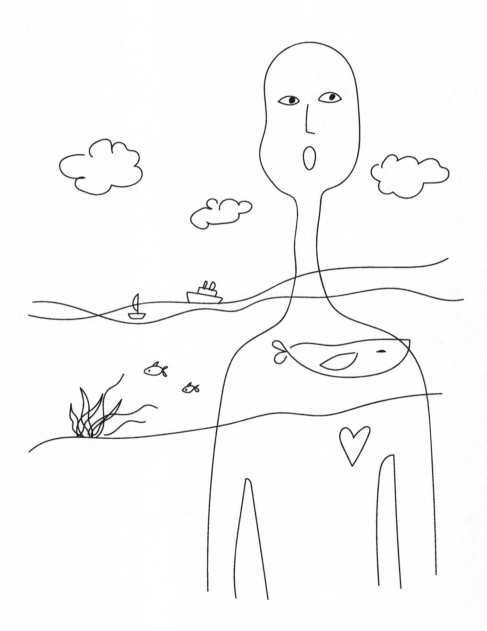

Traumatized love sees the evil
and people who hurt us
through rose colored glasses
So, I am liberating my love
And readjusting my lens

I'm constantly seeking approval

trying to be what everyone else wants

because the only love I know

is love that comes from conforming

to other people's ideas of who I should be

I am worthy of the space I take up

As a human fearfully and wonderfully

made you should never feel sorry for the space you take up

You are here intentionally

so be intentional about the space you consume

Every breath you take

and every fiber of your being

is sewn into the fabric of creation

Without you

the very existence of that which exists

would be marred

your story makes the picture whole

Don't ask a man to write you poetry

That which is seen will become a song

He doesn't write about you because he doesn't see you

Yet and Still

You are magical

you are a song

you are poetry in motion

So, for now

If no one sees you

I see you

and this is your gentle reminder

to write your own poetry

become the song unsung

They Come, and They Go.

Why can't communicating with men be easy?

No need to think
Over process
Guess

Tell me what you want
What you think
How you move

I get my hopes up only to be let down,
but this time, I'm not going to allow it to bother me
My job is to heal, and every moment reminds me
of the work that I must do.

I must find joy in me
I must be at peace with me
I am learning the beauty of rejection and abandonment
at the end of both, I have me.

That is why I must love me with a massive amount of love

אמן

AFFIRMATION

A bilateral root meaning to be firm and to come from a source. To have a pillar of truth or something that stands as a foundation or reminds a person of the support necessary to build a sure foundation. A safe place to anchor or grab hold in a time of need. To nourish and sustain. **מן**

A confirmation or a judgment of self. To whisper or mutter in a low voice and speak to oneself as one speaks to an oracle. From the two-letter bilateral root נא which is defined as a pleading for what is desired or asking for thought or process to be considered and heeded. **נאם**

To depend or rely on something or someone. The process of אמן is one of nurturing and confirmation in truth. One who experiences this word is likened to a skilled worker's sureness of a carefully crafted item. Amen is an intimate process of nurturing and caring for something to make it sure. **אמן**

Affirmations are a confirmatory response to a truth deeply embedded and gifted from the Creator. The Hebrew word for affirmation is amen. It is formed from the bilateral root "mem, nun," which means to be firm and strengthened to continue and operate as a pillar of support to something or someone else. The affirmation practice is seen in the Hebrew cognate "nun, aleph, mem," which means whispering or muttering as if speaking to an oracle or the inner self. The bilateral root of (nun, mem) deepens and simplifies the practice of affirmation into a pleading with the ego to step out of the way to cultivate the true self. The aleph in this word represents the authority of the strong leader for the continuation of mindfulness and an alert, conscious experience. Our affirmations become the groaning of the true self to our ego. The true self asks the ego to step out of the way and give room to the Strong Leader and Creator of breath and Author and Finisher of your faith. Affirmations are the utterance of profound truth or prophecy. When we affirm, we are prophesying the reality of human existence and the endowed power to live according to that truth. This is power, which can only be obtained attached to the Creator of words and truth. Because words are powerful and revealing, we must refrain and train ourselves to speak and rehearse TRUTH.

The patriarch Abraham is the father of affirmative living. He is the first man credited with using affirmations to achieve the right relationship and friendship with the Creator. If you know Abrahams's story, then you know that this was not a process of ease. It took realignment mistakes but ultimately led to him being called the "Father of the Faithful." In like manner, each of us has an open invitation to a life full of blessings and joy if we align and consistently secure ourselves in the truth deeply embedded in each of our hearts and minds.

Keep going

Keep healing

someone needs you to show the way

Lift your gates

No more downcast eyes

No more burdened minds

You are free

You are the generation ushering in the Glory

Practice letting go
Let go of the weight
Let go of the pain
Let go of the thoughts racing in your brain
Emancipate the tension stored in your shoulders
Open your fist

You don't have to fight
You don't have to toil
You are the seed planted in fertile soil
Loosen your jaw
Speak your truth

Release the tears
Release the fear
Release the doubt; your time is here
I know it's hard
I know the weight is heavy
But the baggage you have can't go on this journey

You see we're going up
You see, we're soaring high
You see, the new destination is no longer by and by
No need to wait
The kingdom is within

"Take therefore no thought for the morrow: for the morrow shall take thought for the things of itself. Sufficient unto the day is the evil thereof."
Matthew 6:34 KJV

The past few months have been a mental hamster wheel of epic proportions. I have spun my wheels worrying about the future. The future of this world. The future of my children. The future of EVERYTHING. This week I hit a wall, and instead of trying to climb another mountain or scale the walls of my worry, I was reminded that I have permission to rest at the foot of the mountain. I can pause and lean up against the wall. You see, at the top of the mountain or on the other side of the wall is what's next for us. The wall and the mountain are evidence of Yah's promise. When something stands in front of us, it's not to make us weary, and we don't have to rush because the task is evidence of the promise. Our climb and our journey are the surety of more. I am learning to be gentle on the journey. Gentle with myself and others. Everything you need to move forward is there. If the Creator placed the mountain, he gave you the strength to climb it. Base camp, at the feet of His Majesty, is where we train. Don't forsake the training at the foot of the mountain because it is the quiet moment before the climb that prepares us for the rigor of what is next. Know this; you have the strength, mental clarity, finances, etc., in abundance for TODAY. Tomorrow has enough worries of its own, but it also has its designated provision. The Israelites had to trust Yah daily for provision and deployment in the wilderness. As we walk the wilderness, I challenge each to lean in and rest on the Rock of our Salvation.

Even when you have been uprooted
or have no roots at all
Even when you are simple, strange, and small
You still have breath; you still have life

Even in a window
watching the world move by fast
Even surrounded by bigger plants
that you never will surpass
You still have a purpose; you still must try

Even when the gardener
waters others more than you
And in your mind, you think
He doesn't care for you
You have a place; you have not been forgotten
your time will come; you have an assignment
You must be patient, trust the refinement

Because while others have water

and soil for growth

He gave YOU His breath

so indeed, you matter most

You have the Spirit, something no one can see

It's only made evident

when you proclaim His glory

How do you do that? I'm glad you asked

It's all about commitment

to a singular task

Breathe and Bloom

גבל

BOUNDARIES

To restrain or hinder a strong desire to bring about wholeness. The two-letter כלא root of this word is כל which means to be whole, complete, and tamed for the yoke. The yoke is a task that requires restraint to arrive at a prescribed goal. The goal can be functional relationships, breaking generational curses, or healing, but each goal can only be achieved by the path prescribed by the Master, which is righteousness. The restraining of oneself in the boundaries of the Torah bears the fruit of wholeness (righteousness).

To inscribe, fixing needs into specific parameters or setting a particular portion חוק aside. A boundary is a personal custom that specifies how one wants to function. Boundaries lend specificity to interactions between oneself and others to avoid separation and help build strong bonds. To set a boundary is to develop a compass toward joy and support others in climbing to deeper levels of intimacy without rushing and trauma bonding.

The edge or ends of a region. The edge is the place where the line is drawn, גבל creating a demarcation between what is within one's spectrum or area and what is out of those bounds. This word deals with setting fixed limits, dominion, and rules for remaining within the bounds of a location or mental space. To set a boundary means to understand the restriction. This type of boundary is clear and transparent without ambiguity. This boundary line can be different depending on the relationship, just like territory boundaries may be diverse based on a person's clearance or permissions.

Boundaries are necessary and will come in one form or another. This means that if you do not have boundaries, you will feel like you are being controlled or bound by the actions of others. When a person lacks boundaries, there is the feeling of life happening to you instead of life happening for you or with you. Lack of boundaries leads to haywire in the somatic nervous system and can often be the culprit of mental illness symptoms such as anxiety, depression, paranoia, etc. I posit that many who experience mental dis-ease have never been taught how to create a safe place for themselves in the world by creating boundaries. Creating a proactive game plan for life without triggered responses is possible and imperative. Society believes that learned behavior due to experience, especially trauma, is binding and has permanent ramifications. Well, the Bible doesn't ascribe to that teaching. Humanity is endued with the ability to cultivate and recreate reality, and boundaries create a safe space for that type of restorative healing. The lie that people are bound into circumstances without flexibility is a toxic tactic of the enemy. Still, through the redemptive work of Messiah, freedom allows us to establish boundaries in alignment with our authentic character to make us effective servants of His kingdom.

God established the notion of boundaries in, you guessed it, Genesis. The Creator is the master boundary setter. God set boundaries as soon as the story began. The book of Genesis is full of division and boundaries for creation. Everything has bounds, from the division of day and night to the placing of Adam in a protected garden. Adam's position in the garden came with an instruction to guard the boundary of Eden. Also, He was required to keep the Creator's commandment regarding the restriction on the Tree of Knowledge of Good and Evil to maintain a right relationship with the Creator.

Likewise, we are presently commanded to keep the garden of our minds diligently (Proverbs 4:23). To keep something means to do the necessary work to maintain it. The work of mind "keeping" is deeply rooted in boundaries. The boundaries we set regarding work, family, friendships, and intimate relationships are imperative to ensuring we can serve and obey the Creator's commandments. If boundaries are not fixed and maintained, there is a strong possibility that feelings of loss of "self" will occur, causing a shift into survival mode. In survival mode, we are hyper-vigilant, distrusting, and ineffective at executing the "Fruits of the Spirit" (Galatians 5:22). When we can no longer be practitioners and cultivators of spiritual fruit, we will eventually see diminishing joy, dysfunctional relationships, and loss of neurological stability.

Boundaries are a leading contributor to good mental, emotional, and physical health. Boundaries in relationships are not one-sided; instead, they protect and promote healthy interactions for all parties. Good boundaries help establish clear communication and expectations, which protect from behaviors that cause trauma. This is considered a necessary restraint to the often-insatiable needs and desires of others. When you begin setting boundaries, you will see the restoration of wholeness. The boundary that protects you will also comfort you and cause you to thrive. When you start to feel guilty because setting boundaries can be scary, remember that boundaries are a fundamental element embedded in the fabric of God's creation. The Creator needs you whole for his service, and your boundary is for your sanity, safety, and self-preservation for good works.

My no is not a rejection of you but protection of me. Anyone who says they love you but doesn't want you to protect yourself and your boundaries are lying. To be my best self, I have to have limitations and I can't worry about your feelings

I said yes so, many times
I forgot with each yes
I was saying no to myself

God is an Elohim of Boundaries

When you institute your boundaries, you are living
within your divine right

When I am not welcome, I am quiet

When I am invited to step into a space without confines, I bloom like a flower

I no longer force myself into spaces that don't have the capacity for me.

A boundary is a person's custom, a ritual of sort. It requires specificity of function and instructions for interactions. Boundaries don't limit the beauty of relationship, instead they give unbridled freedom within safe parameters.

Boundaries are for my sanity, safety, and self-preservation.

The only time we feel hurt or angry is when we give up boundaries for the sake of what we think may cause people to treat us better or when we fear negative backlash or punishment. If I have to think about my spouse or friends punishing me, being angry with me for my no then I don't want those people in my life. I don't belong to anyone.

מחשבה

THOUGHTS

A thought is likened to a mental conception. When a woman is impregnated, her body absorbs the fertilized egg into the lining of her uterus to nourish it into a fully manifested human. In like manner, a thought is meditated upon until it is transformed into knowledge and instruction. The only way to develop an idea is to think about it. The mountains to the ancients were a place of thinking and meditation to receive seeds of wisdom from the Divine. Just as the woman's belly rises, giving evidence of an impending birth, the one who climbs the mountain and returns should provide proof of the implantation of spiritual wisdom.

הרה

Thoughts are like a tapestry woven by careful consideration of the expected outcome. The mental design is a blueprint for the manifestation or actualization presented through revelation. A rug is laid down and used as a place to meditate or as a threshold between one dimension and another. In like manner, thoughts are received when we submit to the incorporeal with diligence to transform it into the material.

רג

The holy manuscript teaches, "as a man thinketh so is he." Thoughts are revealed in behavioral inclinations. A person's beliefs shape how they interact with the material world. Thoughts determine one's imaginations, purpose, impulse, propensity and shape the natural disposition. The subconscious is in a constant process of pressing the lived experience like clay. One's frame of mind governs everything perceived and the entire human experience. This frame holds the painting that one's perceived reality paints.

יצר

Thinking about one's thoughts is the only remedy to the error of mindless living. This is not an invitation to obsession; instead, it is a gentle nudge toward self-reflection. When each thought is carefully held and considered without judgment and before acting, a person can begin to redesign their life with intention. When the brain is allowed to wander without a guide or parameter, then life becomes disorganized. With calculated consideration, life can be imagined and designed to join disparate parts into a beautiful masterpiece.

חשב

Trusting Yah in my waking hours like I do when I sleep
Breathing keeps going
The safety of my children

Cares pass away

How can I Trust Yah
 to guide me into my final rest
 if I can't trust him in the land of the living

Oh, that I may trust in Yah
Like an infant that lays swaddled
Sustained and in shalom

That I may grow up
 and be like the weaned child

May I seek Him early and follow him fully
Until my heavy breath drifts into the sleep
that causes my soul to forget the body and safely trust in Him

If We Could See

If we genuinely saw one another through the lens of love,
would we have to resort to sensitivity training
Movements like Black Lives Matter
Stop! Asian Hate!
Would we be transphobic, islamophobic
and fragmented into all the "-isms"
divided

What if we only wanted the best for every person
What if we sought healing of the hate and differences separating
us
Only then could we look deeply at people instead of titles
and love them with compassion, as a person, not as a label

We must stop allowing ourselves to be labeled
Labeled for love
Labeled to conform to chosen similarities
that are decided upon by who?
Instead, Love me for me

No group.

No title.

Label-less Love.

Love me for what's within

Please heal me

Free me from the insecurity

that caused me to abandon me

Box me

for once, can you

see me

without boundaries and borders

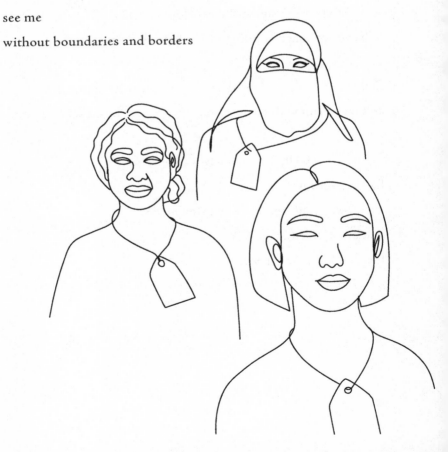

I am the community
and the community is me
The more I cultivate me
The safer the community
The more my inner man becomes a refuge
The more others can seek refuge in the community
The more I love myself
The more abundant in love the community will be

Life is a nightmare and a sweet dream simultaneously

Life is a nightmare, but I am so weary
I can't keep myself from slipping into its horror

Life is a nightmare and a sweet surrender coupled together

The past doesn't want me
the future can't have me
the present has abandoned me
I am a vagabond

Religion destroys reality

The Law of God

The law of God is so perfect and powerful that it only has to be heard
once and creation is required to respond without explanation
The law of God is so perfect that what was not can be with just breath
and vibration
The law of God is so perfect that it is without an audience and will
always be
The Law of God is so perfect that it is life and became life to show love
to all that has life
The Law of God is so perfect that it holds the fabric of the cosmos
together with an immeasurable force yet causes water to
drop light as dew to refresh the most tender plant

The Law of God is so perfect that knees will buckle under its com-
mand, but gentle submission yields a burden that is easy and light

The Law of God is so perfect and under his perfect command I will
remain present because his word is the Power in me to
Transform the imperfection.

the past is afraid to die

because the future is afraid to live

Pure religion

Is love

Mindfulness

Patience

Redemption

& Renewal

If it lacks these things, it is nothing more than a cult

Hey little black boy

Come out to play

It's safe here

Because

I love you

You can't move into tomorrow
until you have financed it with today

Our disobedience causes other people's delay

How painful it must be to be a black man
Your mother wailed at your birth
She mourned you when she laid eyes on you
Your skin was your toe tag

shrills of your beatings fill the halls
Oh, if walls could talk
Lashings borne from fear
and a need to make you hard
'cause this world is ice cold

"Don't baby him" your father said. "He needs to learn to be a man."

You were only 2

You must grow up fast
RUN! the hunters are after you
No! NEVER! Run!
Freeze!
HANDS UP, DON'T SHOOT!

All this love they thought they gave
never softened you
What was for your protection
Now walks the halls of your mind framed as rejection
Ain't no place for a young Hebrew

You grow older but you never heal
from the pain of the miscarriage
that they called your birth

You were born alive
Yet they mourned you as stillborn
Dead on arrival

Look at you
The deepest mahogany hue
Skin fashioned by God
Like a tailor-made suit
Evoking a lullaby called the "sweetest sorrow"
no one wants to tell you
the life you are destined for
makes them wish
you were never born

We call them generational curses
but they should be referred to as generational practices
Unyielding to the toolkit of correction

תורה#

I wonder if the sky knows it's vastness

This boundless ceiling with all its secrets

Each star an unnamed luminary

Depth unknown

Dark but visible

Seducing the world

Beckoning us into the beyond

Telling a story yet remaining a mystery

This twinkling seductress

Continues to captivate me

Telling me the future

As I peer into the past

How could I begin to understand the Infinite

being but a speck staring into the unknown

No one told me that when my womb produced offspring

I would not be a mother

A mourner

A martyr

A mercenary

But not a mother

I would not become a mother

Until I mothered myself

Silence is the Fertile void
Loud but unheard
A speech therapist
Inkwell to the writer's quill
Transforming nothingness into a masterpiece

I used to shudder at the idea of calling myself a writer

Writers are creative

I am merely curious

But I remember the day I became a writer.

I became a writer when fertile lips and fruitful words were
reaped without permission

When orated rhetoric was twisted and stolen for gain

I became a writer when I realized my mind was valuable

and written thoughts could not be used before I had the chance
to speak their truth

I became a writer out of necessity

I became a writer to guard my mind against friend and foe

I became a writer to hear myself and internalize my experience
before sharing

I became a writer because I grew impatient waiting for my turn
to share

So, I WRITE!

The truest love
And true religion
are when we love God without prompt
It's the soul's decision

The Audacity of Humanity

Sometimes I struggle with the audacity of humanity
The audacity to boldly project brokenness out into the world
brokenness that each of us have to bear
yet never taking responsibility for the weight and the pressure
poisoning society with negative emissions
Gross polluters
lewdly baring parts that pervert and subvert true healing

I need a woman's love

The more I neglect myself
the stronger the urge to be loved
creeps inside
I look in the mirror
and there is no softness looking back
I'm becoming calloused
Too many battles fought
Too many scars

I need delicate hands to hold my fragility

I began looking around at the feminine form
Comparing, admiring, but not finding what I am looking for
I wrestle with my thoughts but can't understand what I feel
Am I same-sex attracted?
Can I only get what I need from someone
who experiences the world the same as me
Am I a grown-ass woman
confused about what I want or need
Is this subconscious
is this hidden sin
shadow self getting the best of me
Have I revealed parts
and is this the rest of me

I have to sit with this self as well
I have to pray about a need that could send me to hell
Well...

I must sit with my thoughts
Stop trying to hide from the light
Don't suppress, feel
Feel without guilt
not ascribing sin or labels
Find clarity
Breathe deep and Feel
I fear this process
I am afraid that my same-sex molestation will creep up and reveal to
me something about myself I don't want to know
But I don't push it down.
I breathe through the uncomfortable
I breathe through the thoughts of abomination and shame
I sit with the discomfort of the void
Knowing what I refuse to feel can never be healed
As I wade through the waters of emotion and confusion
I feel something happening
A shadowy figure emerging in the distance
I step closer
My psyche is going to reveal who my desire is for.
I brace myself

As she begins to come closer

I see her feminine silhouette

The light slowly illuminates her face

I gasp

She moves closer

We are nearly face-to-face

She looks familiar

Familial

But I hardly recognize her

She stares deep into my eyes, piercing my soul

Tears stream down my face

And I notice the same on hers

She's begging me

Pleading with me to love her

I reach to grab her

and She reaches back simultaneously

I attempt to secure the embrace

and my hand is met with cold glass

I looked around and realized that I was her and she was me.

Through the darkness of self-discovery

I was not afraid to embrace my duality

I was not looking for someone else

I was the someone else

Calling from deep within

The deep desire for feminine love was for me to release me

To see me

To love me

I am hurt

I am neglected

I am abandoned on the island of my psyche

And no one understands me and my journey like me

I want me

I need me

I am not a lesbian

I am not same-sex attracted

I was by so many other distracted

From seeing me

I yearned for me

I was begging

Beckoning

Me to love me

I was the girl, standing in front of herself, asking her to love her.

LUST/DESIRE

To desire something that is lacking with the same fervor as a necessity like food or water. This need is seen as a void so deep that a person believes without filling this void, they will not survive. The Hebraic definition of lust is also found in an animal's sound when it calls out or pants after its prey or a mate.

אוה

A desire to refine and make tender. A desire to make something or someone delicate and pure. This word deals with pure desire and should evoke thoughts of the garden of Eden. Eden is a place of peace and abundance. It is a place that is cared for, guarded, and cultivated to yield its beauty and potential. Eden is the place of perfect love and harmony. Eden had a system in place that allowed Man and Woman to satisfy one another wholistically. The place where the bone of one's bones and flesh of one's flesh is found. Eden is where the desire and void are filled without perversion and defilement under the Creator's blessing.

עדן

To place a value onto something. When one covets or lusts, they apply worth to something they believe will fulfill a need and then resolutely pursue after the object or person. A person who has material lust believes that looks, finances, or other pleasures can be found in a person or commodity. This appraisal of people and things often causes many to stray from that which is truly valuable. Seeking things status and becoming ambitious to fill voids caused by trauma.

המד

The strike of a serpent. To draw from someone or take mentally, physically, and emotionally. This word can also be translated as milk. For instance, when a child feeds from its mother's breast, it draws on her body as the source for its nourishment. When a person is immature in their desire, they will seek relationships to extract and often leave others feeling drained and used.

שפה

When a baby cries, the method of soothing the child is to bind or swaddle them to feel secure. This process silences their insecurity and brings comfort. In genuine desire, a bond is formed, and a loving connection is fostered. When people have a secure attachment, they contribute calmness to the inner being of those with who they surround and create relational bonds.

חשק

The word lust (אוה) immediately evokes thoughts of untamed sexual energy and inner turmoil. A lustful person is seen as struggling to keep their want and desire for others under control. People every day are struggling to remain monogamous, faithful, and pure, but what if the word lust was alluding to more than just carnal desire. I posit that sexual desire and physical attraction are not the root cause of lust. It's a very superficial view of what it means to lust, and therefore many people find it so hard to overcome this particular issue. In Greek, the word is ἐπιθυμία (epithymia) means to desire; lust; crave. These words are abstract because they don't tell what a desire is, what lust is, and what a person is craving. Abstract definitions leave each word to be defined by the individual's lived experience or personal conviction. This makes the Greek language a gateway but not the destination to the concrete linguistic function of lust found in the Hebrew language.

Hebrew is an action-based language that highlights the process and then remedies the negative and positive charges of word meanings. There are different words for lust in the Hebrew language because lust is a term with different meanings depending on the function or dysfunction of relational interactions. Lust in the Hebraic sense is not just sexual desire as the English word would like one to believe. Lust can be the desire or will of a person to go after things or people or covet. Lust causes a person to want to take what belongs to someone else or use people or material things to fill a void in their lives. Also, lust can be the desire to love, bind, and nurture a person tenderly to bring refinement. Each of these meanings gets its direction based upon a person's, אוה which means functional or dysfunctional desires. When the desire is within the Creator's function, there is beauty and pleasure. When the desire is dysfunctional and is an alternative path than that prescribed by the Creator, there is pain and sin.

Lust of the flesh is also how people choose their own will and path over the Creator's. When personal desires and goals are before healing and transparency with the Source, there will always be a deep void. Avoiding the call to refinement and wholeness is the ultimate root cause of relational dysfunction. There comes the point where past hurts and traumas have to be handed over to break cycles of brokenness. If the shattered pieces are not surrendered, pain and anguish will infiltrate every area of a person's life.

When a person has unhealed trauma and voids caused by dysfunction, their desires are dysfunctional. Often the very thing that causes the pain for the broken becomes their go-to remedy and becomes the direction where their will is focused. Self-will creates a defect in the soul. The soul howls out in pain for the hollow void to be healed, but carnality is in the driver's seat. Appeasement of the flesh attracts a carbon copy of suppressed hurt. In these instances, the abused become the abuser and vice versa. They are therefore tossed into a cycle of depletion and being depleted. Enslavement to the flesh ensues to supply the next fix or temporarily fill for the desolation. It is the responsibility of those who are called to the path of righteousness and refinement to reflect, introspect, and cry out to have our souls filled so that we can align our desire with the Father's will.

When I am sick you rejoice

When you are ill, I give my wholeness to bring you to life

Your wholeness is my sickness

Yet I sacrifice myself a million times

because being sick is better than being lonely

I loved you but I couldn't be near you

You were fire

And I

Tender

You destroyed what was left

Remember last time I rebuilt

And I welcomed your flame

to warm my lonely heart.

When is enough, enough

Another hit

Another high

Letting him rest between my thighs

Another rendezvous to risk it all

More guilt

More shame

More whispering of your name

Private choices

Public humiliation

When will the bondage you are in reach a point

where you call out for redemption?

A hole so deep nothing can escape

Victims caught in the web

In this story I am the hunter

And they are the prey

"If you won't someone else will"

Until…

There are secrets and lies

A relationship broken

Be careful what you wish for

Guard your mouth

These are not idle words to be spoken

She is the woman of folly
Beckoning men to her table of death
Feasting on their admiration to fill her emptiness
She cries out "my husband is away"
Scenting his sheets for her rendezvous
Covering lies with accusations
Paranoid because of twisted deception
Walking past mirrors hiding from her reflection
She wonders if he sees through her
She questions who she has become
But after 5 shots and a glass of wine
The ritual begins
She's hungry for attention
She's empty
And his rejection makes this easy

Only Yah can fill this black hole

The Beauty of My Anxious Heart

A heart that once beat rapidly
Chasing the temporary sweetness of lust
now aches at the thought of transgression

Shield my eyes from lust
Guard my heart against froward and haughty thinking

I would instead remain humble in the gravel then cause shame
once again to your name

When my sins were secret, you concealed and covered me
You brought me into the chamber of chastisement where I was
disciplined and refined
Although I broke my promise, you never broke me

Attraction is not love

Erections
Wet and throbbing projections don't equal
love

Penetrations
Heart skips and palpitations are not love

I have a type
healing, like me

LOVE

The following words give us love in their entirety. While each person may experience love differently, love should encompass each of these components to be considered a replicable expression. Each word expresses love in either a romantic, familial, or universal manner. But it should be noted that the love for a man to a woman should encompass the entirety of the love definitions because it is the love between the pillars of humanity that sets a precedent for all other love experienced in the world. As you read the words and explore the qualities of divinely inspired love, I want you, the reader, to think about how the flaws of understanding can skew the expression of love. I want you to explore how the withholding of love can cause the heart to wax cold, but how the flame of passion can melt the hardest of stone, creating an eruption of lava that will cool, creating mountains and new foundations. I hope that through this journey of love, you understand why love is the highest form of religion and a necessary component like air and water for the survival of humanity.

Two danglers, breasts, or an aphrodisiac. Breasts are the love fruit of the woman's body. They are the place of passion and nourishment supporting the needs of the fruit of her womb and her husband. Best evoke feelings of safety, security, and sensuality. For a child, the breast holds the milk and serves as a place to be sustained, grow, be comforted, and be nourished. In like manner, the breast of a man's wife provides the same safety and security. Unfortunately, modern culture rejects the security that a man finds in his wife's bosom due to toxic masculinity and breast only being a place of desire instead of refuge. A man is commanded by scripture (Proverbs 5:19) to leave his father and his mother, and because the Creator knew man needed comfort in His infinite wisdom; he gave him the woman. In doing so, a man finds the safety of a nurturer and the passion of a lover in the breast of his beloved. In the same way, a woman necessitates the safety and love that she leaves behind in her parents' home. The beloved's love is passionate, safe, and rooted in reciprocity.

דוד

The bilateral root word for אהב is הב which means to look to the house in awe and provide. This provision is physical, but it also means providing whoever is under one's care with what they need to be whole and prosperous. This is not just shelter, but security, friendship, affection, and consistency in presence. Having someone to love is a privilege. It is a gift from the Creator to express the essence of his being to creation. Love is more an assignment than a feeling. Love is a complete devotion to the object of one's affection. Most people see love as something that comes naturally, but the scripture has several commandments on loving our spouses, families, communities, and the broader spectrum of creation.

אהב

Love is protection. When one gives their love, it is implied that they are offering their protection. Protection from those who will try and hurt those they love, but maybe more importantly from the parts of themselves that can bring hurt and pain. This type of love is a burning love for the beloved and against those who seek to quench it. Because of this, the one providing the love becomes a place of refuge. Just like the breast of the woman is a place of refuge, the bosom of the man is a place where the woman can be held close and cherished. She knows that in his arms, she is safe, and then there is a wall up between her and the world, and he is committed to keeping people and things out that will disrupt her mentally, physically, and emotionally. The man becomes the brooding hen like the Creator who will destroy anyone who seeks to upset the peace of his beloved.

חבב

The man or shepherd watches closely to protect and feed the flock. In like manner, love has to be managed and tended to. Love cannot happen without intentionality and communion. Lovers must keep company with one another. When the shepherd leads the sheep into the pasture and returns them home, trust is built. During a relationship, when the man watches the woman and leads her the same trust is built. In families and with children, it is in the moments when parents are tender and give themselves grace and permission to change for the better that strong bonds are built. Like the sheep come to the shepherd for safety, those around one who shows love to themselves, and others will be called upon for physical sustenance and spiritual guidance.

רעה

Through affection, individuals are bound together. Physical affection is necessary for building strong, loving relationships. When we love someone, we desire to hold them close. We want to embrace them. A hug is not a simple act of affection, but rather it provides an encircled, safe place with someone we trust and have built a relationship. When we hug, we create pillars in the world that turn us inward to one another and place our hearts together in a close communion

חשק

Lust is a necessary component of romantic love. Lust is often viewed negatively because it is misused to illicit sex out of the marriage covenant, but lust in marriage is likened to flirting. Lust is like a musical instrument with sensuous tones beckoning the lovers together to wonder, marvel, and become astonished with one another. The build-up to love-making and intimacy is a part of keeping the flame of love awake. Lovers should continue to seek one another's hearts and affection for the duration of their intimate unions.

עגב

אֲנִי לְדוֹדִי וְדוֹדִי לִי הָרֹעֶה בַּשּׁוֹשַׁנִּים

I am my beloved's, and my beloved is mine: he feedeth among the lilies.
Song of Solomon 6:3

I don't believe in reincarnation

But I often have this eerie feeling
that there was once a deep connection
between me and a lover from a past life

And now every day I am chasing the high of this love
My experience tells me I have yet to find it
 but it feels so close I can taste my loves lips on mine.

In the next life
We become
What we lacked
You are the wind
And I am the lotus

You are the sunrise
And I the full moon

We are indispensable
We are always present

We never lose one another
Because
We are
one

I feel guilty for not being able to teach you love

I can teach with eloquence and clarity

but can't find words to draw a map

to the love that I have for you.

Warm sun and a crisp gentle breeze
Lovers in love
steam floating from 4-dollar coffee
deep sighs and jazz
the pensively enamored couple
surrender to the moment

she writes
he researches

they exchange layered smiles
waiting for time
to continue
standing still in the stolen moment

Don't love me with all that you have or are

Love me with the infiniteness that God is

Love me beyond

Beyond you

Beyond me

Pass over me with your love and love God

All I ask is to be allowed the crumbs that fall from divine loves table

I am quirky like

Khaki shorts and shirts that are tucked in

Like hot cocoa on ice, but don't call it chocolate milk

Like late-night rambling about orange juice and 9-volt batteries

My type of sexy is bleached sweats and cowboy boots

I like basketball video games and Nikki Giovanni poems

My dance moves are lousy

and awkward silence is music to my melancholy

I can be

A mind full of contradictions and oddly decisive

A walking anomaly and freakishly pensive

Independent but fueled by affection

Vocal and quiet

Like now

at a loss for words

So here I stand

In the doorway of your heart

Awkward, trying my best to give sexy vibes

Wondering if I should walk over and kiss you

I stumble over my feet

Still giving confidently goofy energy

Offering all of me

in lacy lingerie and mixed matched socks

A particular kind of heaven
this last month has been nothing short of such
part peculiar rather absurd
yet the way I feel is quite divine
something about the new space
and renewed time is other worldly
the way you hold me
touch me
and look at me
takes my breathe away
what a golden hour
what a privilege
even in its peculiarity
I want to normalize
the rarity of
paradise

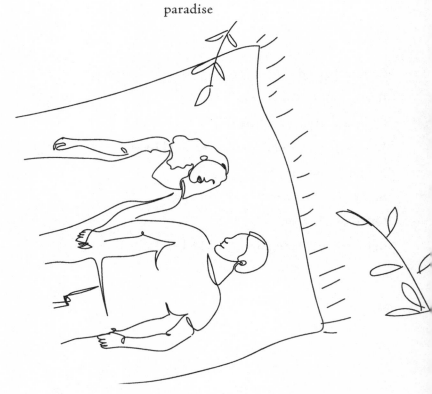

I awake with the taste of you still lingering on my lips
The way the sun creeps through my window and touches my skin
floods my memory of where your hands have been
I feel you in everything
Everywhere

Your love has humbled me

You touch me gently

Hidden away I am nourished in the wilderness of our love

You whisper in my ear

Anything and everything is yours

You look in my eyes

Gifting me the future and erasing the past

You beckon me to my call

You grant me my petition

You promise restoration

God promises restitution

You open your lips and out comes healing

Ask me queen, give me your request, unto half the kingdom is yours

Like the myrtle who experiences the twisting affliction of growth

I stand like Queen Esther

Meek and humble

Leading to follow

Love me creatively
Love me like an artist observing the world
for inspiration concerning his next masterpiece

Study me like you can find the cure for cancer
or eternal life in my every movement

Touch me like there is invaluable treasure buried beneath my skin
Make love to me like there is healing found between my thighs

Explore my minds like the depths of a vast ocean
Paint love on the canvas of my heart
that is on display for the world to see

Bring forth a masterpiece that encapsulates
the never-ending adventure
and inspiration that is our love

DIVORCE'S EPITATH

When you left, you took my love with you
When you returned, you brought my life with you

יאשיהו

ABOUT THE AUTHOR

Huldah writes.

Made in the USA
Coppell, TX
17 March 2022

75149186R00100